THE SCIENCE OF KUNDALINI

Lifes Recipes

James Gilbride

James Gilbride

MIND BODY
REPROGRAMMING

THE SCIENCE OF KUNDALINI

"LIFE Recipes"

Transformation

INTRODUCTION

What you will find in this book is multiple exercises
to train the body and mind to work in coherence to
give you a New Life from the one you know of.
The book is filled with exercises from kundalini
also known as the Mother of all Yoga.

The motions of the exercises are more for the body's conditioning working on the internal body outwards.

Now this book is not just a deeper understanding of Kundalini exercises. It comes with the Science and a breaking down has been done on the exercises.

Now some will be hard still to adapt to, but if you remember the forum isn't so important.

The forum comes with practice the same as most things in the material world for the body to adapt to.

What's important is being aware of the senses your using and how your connecting to the Mind using the senses.

The wholeness of everything in the book is to create your life in serval different types a way depending on what you're looking for.

The main thing is helping to reach a higher consciousness in multiple ways with different exercises in the direction for your desires.

Each exercise can help you reach that higher Consciousness in the area of the Kundalini intention and having your intent behind it.

Science shows today that we can reach a higher consciousness with awareness and this is how kundalini works.

Kundalini has more to it though, with the exercises known as Kriya's.

It builds the body internally preparing it for the higher consciousness as if you were just to reach the higher consciousness unprepared it could be overwhelming.

This is where Kundalini has a negative that runs alongside it.

I'm sure you've heard for every negative there's a positive like a battery.

You can't have one without the other.

That's the case here, looking from the science side
Kundalini is not harmful in any way even if you pushed
yourself so hard to pass out it wouldn't be negative it
would be only a release of energy you were not ready for
and you would still get a wonderful experience.

Obviously, you don't want to push that far as it's
scary to the unknown, as you read it you got a fear,
I'm sure and that's what Kundalini is for.

It will bring about your fears and what's holding you back in
life so you can let go of them and this is that negative side.

A lot of people aren't willing to deal with the past and when
Kundalini reaches the higher consciousness Gates let's just say.

Before you go through those gates you have to let go
of all your past that's been holding you back.

Know that things will come up, so you can Finally let go
and move forward in life to being who you want to be.

"Emotional Times"

So be prepared or do not go on any further.

So be prepared or do not go on any further.

So be prepared or do not go on any further.

I repeat that as it's so important if you're not managing
life very well now you might find it very difficult
to overcome any emotions that arise.

Were you would be advised to work with a teacher!

This goes to anyone who finds something that
arises that's difficult to overcome.

It's the Knowing why it came about even
if you hadn't remembered it.

Now is the time to realise it Showing you it was there all a time.

This was a belief you had programmed in to your

system (Subconscious Mind) and higher consciousness
is showing it to you that you have this here.

Now will you let it go it's asking, so you let it go, by seeing it
as the past and you are not in the past no more. You've moved
on to being a stronger being as you are now in the NOW.

So, this is the Negative effects of Kundalini.

Reaching the higher consciousness, you have to be willing
to Clear the past as you've known it and just let go and
move forward and enjoy what follows after that.

What Follows after that is leaving your past life behind
you as you knew it. The one that didn't serve or satisfy
you in a fulfilling way. Which is why you searched
for more and this Book can give that to you.

When you can pass by who you are, you can become
a better version of yourself.

You will see the world differently and have more of a true
understanding of everything and how everything is connected.

You will come in contact with a higher force
and an understanding of who you are.
You will Know your true purpose of why you are here.

You will be able to guide yourself down the path that you
desire and find the life that you've been longing for.

Make Sure You want to Change Before moving forward and
understand it won't be easy but when you get there it will
have been more then worth the journey. You will wonder
how you never seen the world the way it truly is.

You will be able to enjoy Life.

GUIDE

All exercises are aimed to use your senses and activate meridians in the body which go on to Activate energy points in the body.

In return will rise the spinal fluid up your spine hitting the pineal gland sending it a message of your intention from how you've activated your senses.

I've broken down some of the kundalini but some exercises may still be challenging to some.

The idea behind it all is to have belief in what you're doing. Your intention by activating the senses and working with the mind is what's important not so much as perfecting the exercise.

As when you reach higher consciousness you will see how perfect you already are.

Being aware of the Breath and the abdomen pulling to the spine as you say mudras is a lot more important than any of the physical movement of the body during exercise.

The exercise is more for preparing you for better energy flow which is highly recommended, as you don't want a lot of things coming up at once to deal with as I said it can be overwhelming.

So, a breakdown of everything

Exercise, Belief with intention, Breath Awareness and body Awareness of the Abdomen and the Spine.

Knowing this and putting it together as a wholeness.

You can bring in your own exercises if you

find these to hard or demanding.

Just remember these exercises are here to push you. If you don't keep yourself pushed hard then how will you succeed in anything.

Last thing before Entering in to the kriya's Know that you do not need to do all them they all have different meanings and intentions behind them.

They are a list of different ones to help you manage your way through life when needed.

Recommended to always keep practicing in the weaker areas of your life and when you reach higher consciousness you can keep there by keeping up the practice and not getting lost in the material world.

LEARNING TO MEDITATE

Apply Jalandhar bandh (at the end of the book(body locks))

Sitting with your spine straight close the eyes and bring them to focus between the eyebrows turning them in and up.

Repeating SAT NAAM.

Pressing the 4 fingers of the right hand on the left wrist feeling the pulse with each fingertip as you press lightly.

Mentally feel the words SAT NAAM from the heart as it beats and flow with it as you repeat the words out.

Starting with 11 minutes and working way up to 30 or more.

This is good for someone who doesn't know how to meditate or never meditated before.

MALA MEDITATION

Reducing Stress and enhancing Wisdom, Patience and Health

This is a set of beads either 108,54 or 27 beads
traditionally kept on a silk tread with one bead larger
than the others which is called the Guru bead.

The larger bead is found where the tassels hang and
the tassels represent a thousand lotus petals.

What it is doing is keeping your senses in place
with your awareness of this material object as
a connection to none material forces.

Meditating with Mala with different fingers will connect
with different parts of the brain you stimulate meridians
and connect to the organs sending signal to the brain.

Index finger: Wisdom, Knowledge and Prosperity

Middle finger: Enhances patients

Ring finger: Promotes health, Vitality and strengthens
the Nervous system

Little finger: Communication Skill and intelligence

How to use Mala is to hold with either hand. Start by holding
the bead next to the Guru bead, rolling through the beads
as you repeat your mantra and adding any prayer you wish.
Keep rolling through the beads bringing them towards the
body as the Guru bead ascends downwards and around.
When you get to the guru bead your mantra is finished. To
start again you turn the beads round and go the opposite

way repeating your mantra and any prayer you have.

Example: SAT NAAM you would move one bead for each word. WHA-HAY GUROO move only one bead.

Saying the two together SAT NAAM WHA-HAY GUROO move only one bead.

You can use any mantra or affirmations while saying to yourself or out loud. Out loud being more of a vibration through sound.

Can be done at any time when walking around through your day or a deep meditation.

Listening to your mantra and feeling it and how it is affecting the body. In meditation you can focus on the third eye in the centre of the eyebrows.

https://www.google.com/url?
sa=i&source=images&cd=&cad=rja&uact=8&ved=2ahUKEwjQ7-uVhKnnAhVr8-
AKHRkgAPoQjB16BAgBEAM&url=https%3A%2F%2Ffree-spirit-
shop.com%2Fproducts%2F108-natural-black-onyx-7-chakra-mala-bead-
necklace&psig=AOvVaw3WfQZ7qz_bQm_TBPoLmCWP&ust=1580394954730993

AAD NAAD KRIYA

Clear Your Language,

The Secret Power Of The Knowledge.

Posture & Mudra

Sit up with your spine straight.

Interlock the fingers together with your writing hand
index finger over the other index finger.

Palms of the hands are connected

and the thumbs are together. Stretching back the thumbs

Keeping them pointed up. Relax the arms down by

your sides. The forearms are pulled into the chest.

The hands Should now be just below the heart feeling

it beat of your thumbs.

Now Breath.

Deeply inhale and completely exhale as
you Chant the mantra, Once.

Close the Eyes.

Now chant the Mantra as you Exhale the breath completely.

RAA RAA RAA RAA

MAA MAA MAA MAA

SAA SAA SAA SAT

HAREE HAR HAREE HAR

Duration of 9 minutes.

Ending with a deep inhale and holding the breath at

least 15 seconds building on this and Exhaling
through the mouth.

Repeat 3 times.

You can

extend the time up 60 minutes or longer depending
or your desire.

BALANCING THE AURA

This exercise is for building physical energy and stamina.

Strengthening of the Navel (Energy Centre).
Rhythmically moving

the energy from Navel to the Crown Energy Centre and back.

The flowing of energy awakens and energies of all energy
centres between the navel and the crown.

In result lighting up your Aura around you.

You can become to master with practice and will become
a very delightful exercise expanding on that Aura.

1) Sit crossing your legs or comfortable if unable to cross legs.

Pointing your elbows out to your sides. So, your
upper arms are parallel to the floor.

Crossing hands in front of your eyes (Open or
Closed).

Separating your fingers wide apart like a web.

Keeping the arms parallel stretching the upper arms
apart as the hands come away from each other.

Then bringing them back again.

Continue the exercise for 3 minutes being
rapid and forceful in the motion.

With Eyes open you get to hit the visual senses.

With closed you bring about more awareness of
the bodies motion heightening your awareness.

2) Come in to Archer Pose, with the right leg

In front of the left with the left leg

straight back your foot should be flat on the
floor at a 45° angle to the right foot.

Holding the right arm straight out front keeping parallel to the
ground while making a fist and with the thumb pointing up.

Holding the left arm back as if your holding
a bow pulling back on the string.

All the way back to the shoulder.

Facing direction of the front foot and eyes focused
just above the fist.

Now begin to drop the right knee dropping the
body down and then coming back up.

This exercise should be done 2 minutes each
side Switching feet around.

Do in a powerful and rhythmically flow.

BALANCING THE AURA PART 2

3) Moving in to Cobra Pose. Lie down on

your stomach with the palms flat on the

floor directly under the shoulders.

Having the soles of your feet pointing upwards.

Arching the spine from the crown to the base of
the spine till your arms are straight.

Pushing up with the buttocks in to a Triangle Pose while
supporting yourself on your palms and soles of your feet.

Keeping straight lines at first will be difficult
but with the practice you will get the straight
lines performing the perfect Triangle.

Now returning back to Cobra Pose, moving back and
forth between poses for a time of 5 minutes.

4) Come to cross legs or sitting comfortably till you can cross your legs
but always keeping back straight.

Sit and Meditate pulling in on the muscles of the

rectum, sex organs and Navel area and relaxing
them again, Pulsating for 2mins.
Come to relax and meditate sense the body and when you've

sensed the body and became aware repeat for a further 2minutes pulsating and then coming back to relax.

Finishing of pulsating once again after you've sensed the body.

At the end of the pulsating pull everything up with a deep breath holding it till comfortable to release.

Exhale forcing out from the navel area and holding again till comfortable to come back to your natural breathing.

You should practice from 15 minutes up to 60minutes.

This exercise Moves energy between your energy centres and aura back and forth clearing all energy paths to your Aura.

Practice will bring perfection.

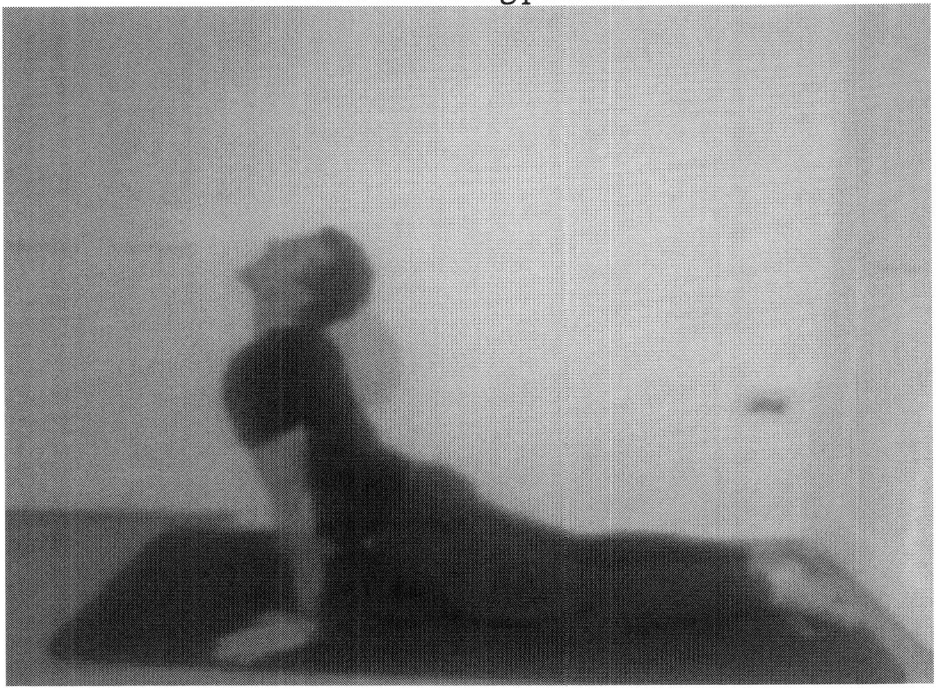

BREATH OF FIRE
WITH LION'S PAWS

(Apply jalandhar bandh at the end of the book (body locks)).
Resetting the Brain's Electromagnetic Field

Crossed legged or whatever is comfortable always keeping back straight.

Mirroring a Lion's Paws: curling and tighten the fingers
of each hand.
Try to keep focus on the tension in the
hands throughout the exercise.

Extending both of your arms out to the sides, parallel to
the ground with the palms facing upwards.

Bringing both arms over the head with the
hands passing over the crown of

the head crossing each other. Leaving the palms facing
downwards.

Then bring back to the original position again.

Continue in a rhythmic forum.

Switching which hand is in front doing both sides
equally while breathing with the arms in motion.

Continue the exercise at a fast pace in haling as arms
extend and exhaling as they cross over the crown.

Breathing in and out the nose with breath
of Fire very quick breathing forcing out
the breath with the navel area.

Continue for 2 minutes building up to 10 minutes.

Finishing off Without breaking the flow of the exercise,

stick your tongue out and down all the way and
keep going for another 15 seconds.

Then inhale bringing the tongue in placing the arms
at 60 degrees, so that they form an arc around

the Crown. The palms Should be facing
down kept apart over the head.

Holding the breath for as long as comfortable to release.

Keep the arms fixed in position as you exhale the
breath and hold once again till comfortable.

Repeat inhaling and holding till comfortable and
Exhaling and holding till comfortable.

Now come to relax, Meditate at

the Heart Centre relaxing your hands down by
your sides or also can place on the heart.

Following the natural flow of the breath.

Listen to an uplifting song and sing with it while relaxing.

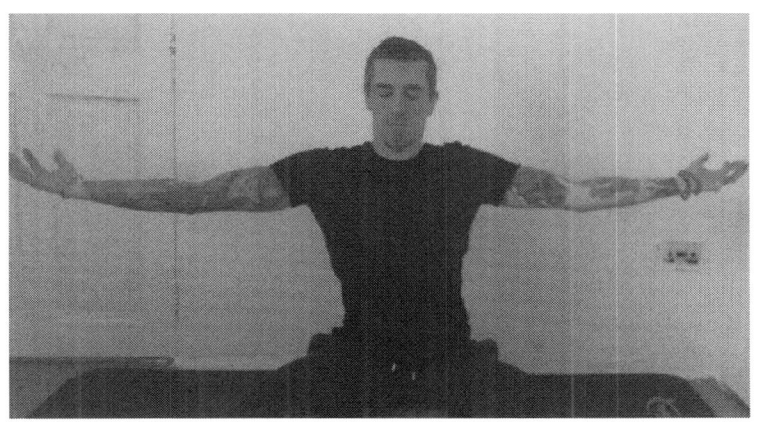

This short kriya has a powerful effect on the brain

and its electromagnetic field. The hand position

triggers Energy paths to all areas of the brain.

The movement of the arms moves the lymph in

the lymphatic system. Also, the nervous system

is challenged to change its current state.

The Breath of Fire pumps more oxygen to the lungs
to give more healthy blood flow and pulsating the
spinal fluid up the spine to the pineal Gland.

Increasing your frequency and connection to everything.

FOR A STABLE SELF

(Apply jalandhar bandh at the end of the book (body locks))

Sitting in a comfortable position working to crossed legged.

Keeping the eyes slightly open or can close and focus at the centre of the brow point.

Holding the right hand in front of the body at the level of the throat curling the fingers into a fist.

Keeping the thumb held back. Holding
the left hand directly below

the right fist. Curl the fingers of the left hand into a firm fist keeping the thumb held back.

The left-hand tip of the thumb should be about 2inches from the bottom of the right hand.

You should be covering the area of your Diaphragm
to your mouth.

Keeping your forearms parallel to the ground.

Follow the natural pattern of the breath then inhaling deeply and quickly and then exhale immediately, powerfully.

Keeping the neck locked in position the thumbs held up.

Hold the breath out for count of 26 seconds doing this you should feel the navel area pulling in tight to the spine.

Visualize as your counting and feel the energy moving up the spine with your awareness.

Moving up each vertebra by the count of one is the first vertebra at the base of the spine, working up to the 26 Vertebra at the top of the spine where it connects to the skull.

Continue for 2-15 minutes.

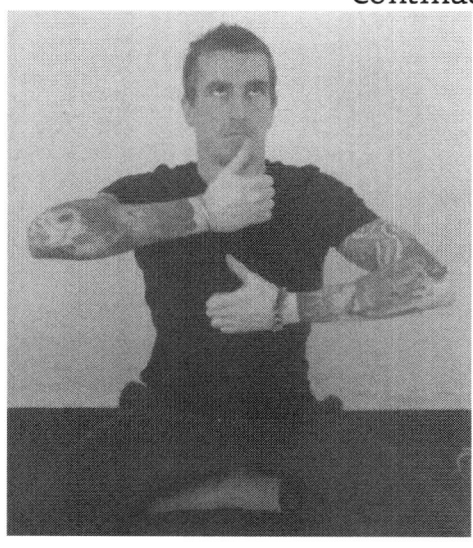

The main effect of the meditation is to increase the sense of self.

Increasing good judgement and eliminating Negative

Thoughts and feelings.

We've often fears that makes us jumpy and irregular taking us away and over powering our inner self.

Removing your fears from the ego and being steady connected to self.

BLESSING GUIDANCE
BY INTUITION

(Apply jalandhar bandh at the end of the book (body locks))

Sitting spine straight keeping eyes Slightly open or closed.

Extending the arms up in a circular arch so the palms face down just above the crown of the head. Keeping the hands separated around 12 inches with the spread out from the fingers letting them hang loosely.

Inhaling and exhaling 8 equal breaths with each inhale and exhale repeating

SAA-TAA-NAA-MAA 8 times on the inhale
and 8 times on the exhale.

Continue up to 11 minutes and then you can
build on the time to your comfort.

Don't go past 31 minutes.

Ending with a deep inhale while raising your arms over the
head keeping the arms Stretched backwards and upwards.

Roll the head back looking up. Putting full force
into it Stretching out the spine.

Releasing the breath on exhale relaxing the
arms and then repeat the breath 2 more times
stretching the arms and the spine on each breath.

Now relax.

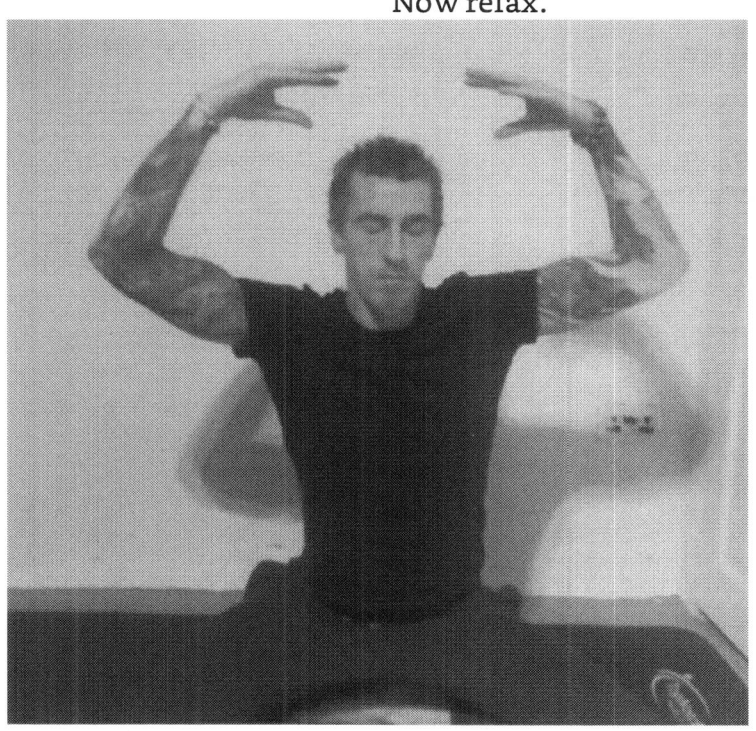

This meditation takes practice to perfect don't expect
to get the first time.

Your arms may become painful after time goes passes.

When this happens bring your attention to the breath letting
any images and sensations in the arms dissolve away.

This Will stimulant the pineal and pituitary glands
and in result gaining an increase in intuition.

Intuition corrects our judgements from the psychic realms.

This meditation teaches you to be still and
to see the real from the unreal.

Taking the fantasy out of the imagination guiding you.

HIGH TECH
YOGA KRIYA

Sit with the spine straight and eyes closed.

Time: 127 minutes.

1. Thumb to

index finger

wrists resting on

knees with palms

facing up.

2. Hands resting on the lap with palms up.

3. Thumb to middle finger pressing fingers into the navel area.

4. Thumb to ring finger pressing fingers into heart centre.

5. Thumb to little finger pressing the other fingers of hands below ears between the side and back of the neck.

6. Both hands covering the face with fingertips by the hairline.

7. Interlocking your fingers on top of your

head.

8. Extending the arms straight out at 45 degrees with your palms facing up to the sky. Repeat the Mantras as you flow through the sequence Translated in English under each Photo.

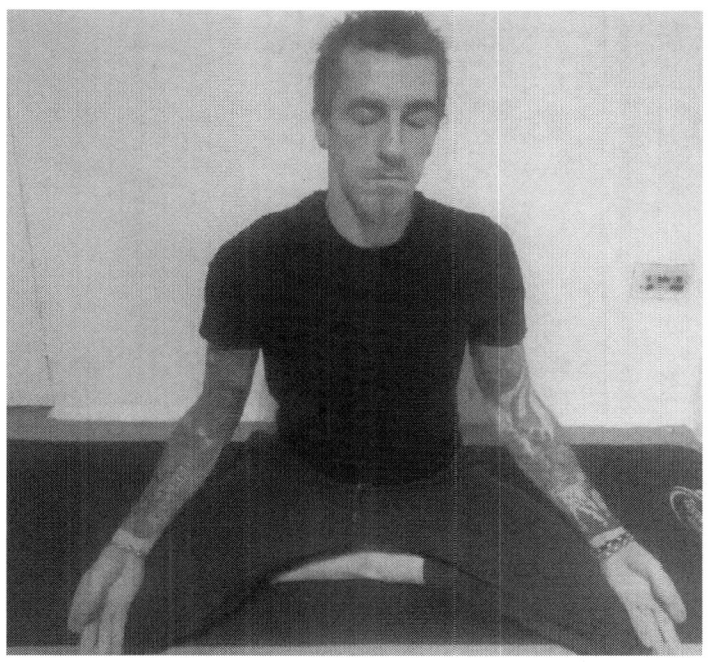

God Himself is looking out for us.

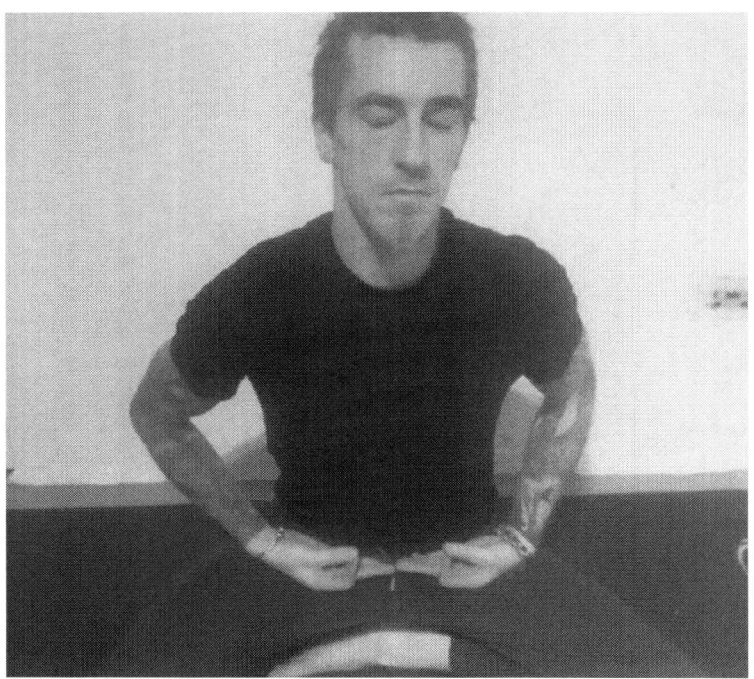

Gives us the light, and takes care of our affairs.

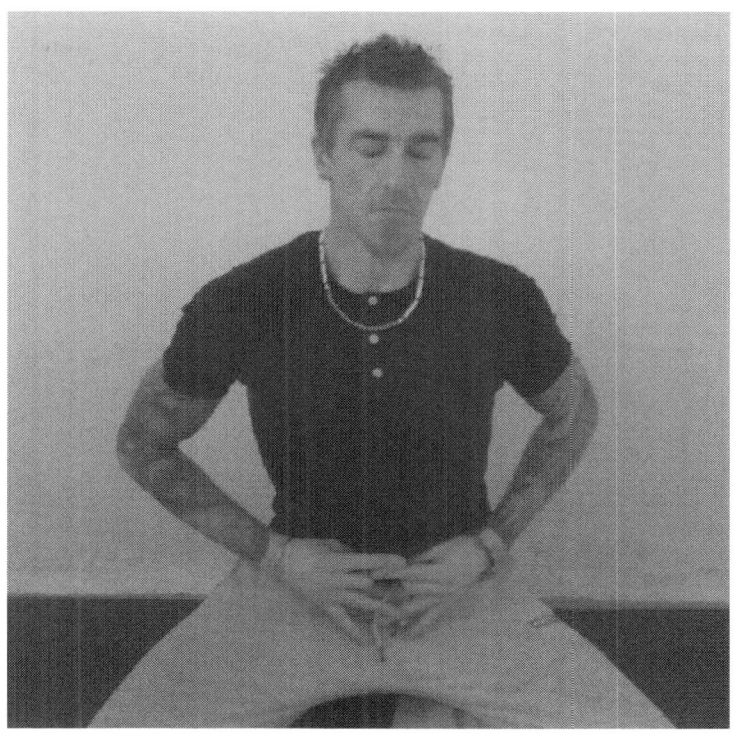

God is merciful, and never forgets us.

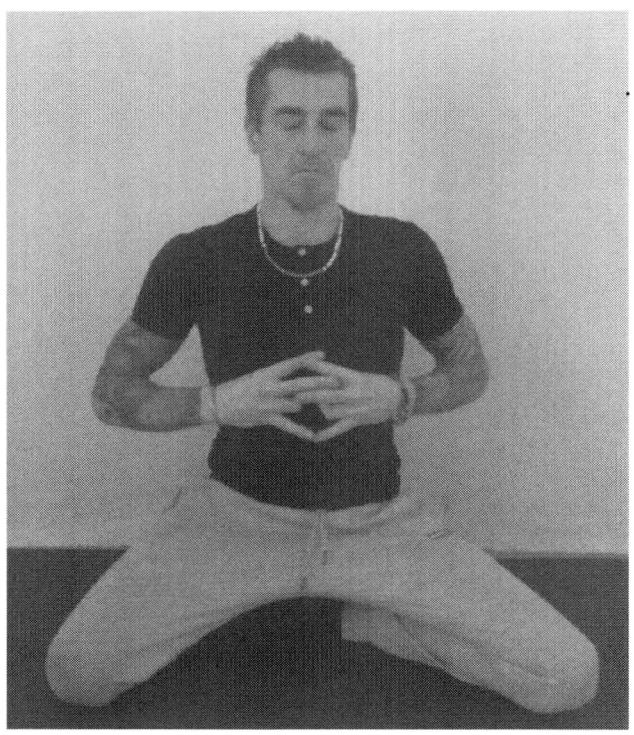

God guides us, giving us good people to help us.

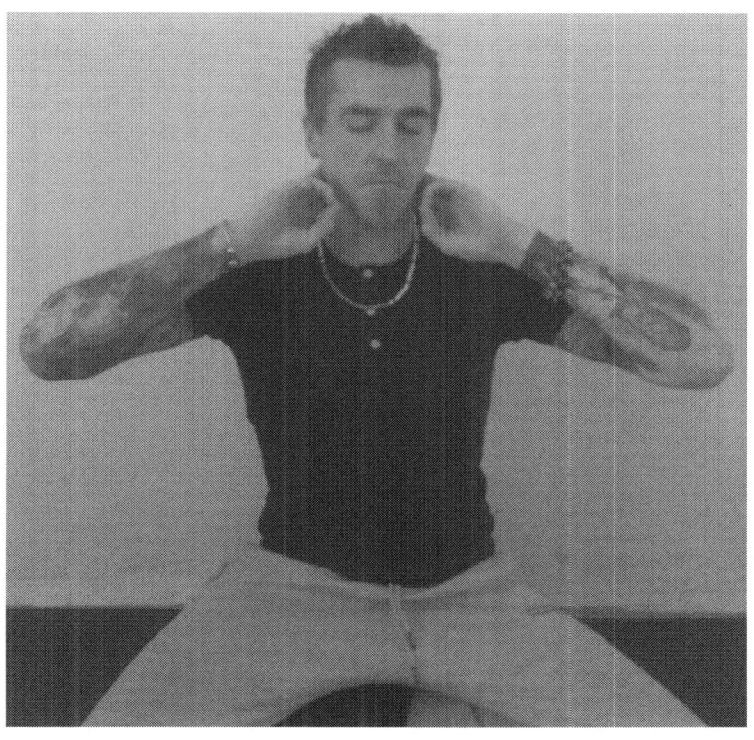

God does not allow hurt to come to us.

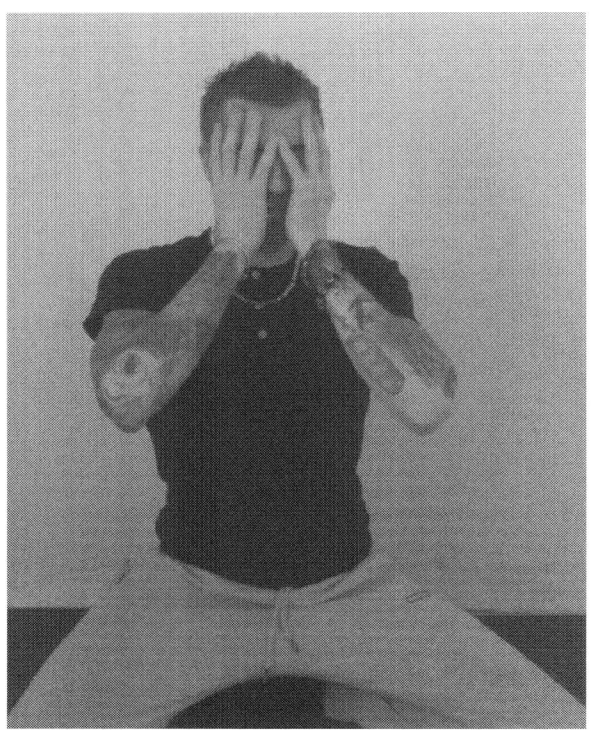

I take comfort in the thought of God.

When I remember God,

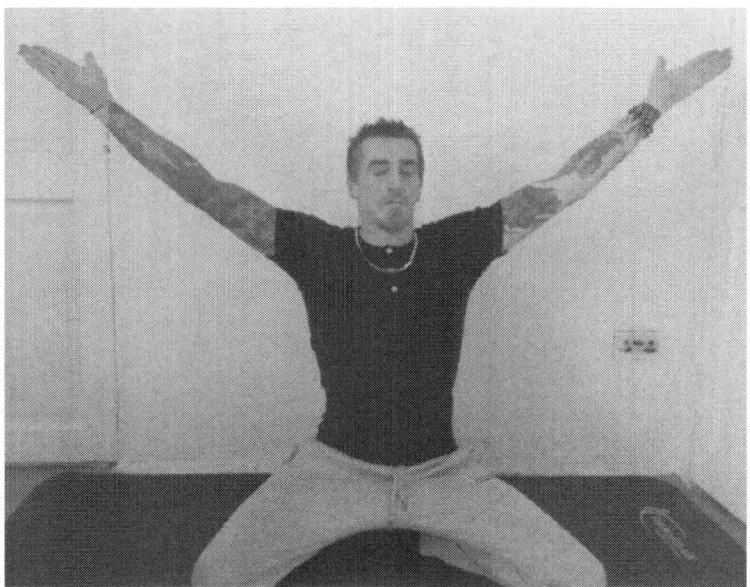

I feel peaceful and happy and all my pain departs.

KIRTAN KRIYA

Bring a total Mental Balance

Sitting with the spine straight eyes closed focusing on the centre of the Brows.

Repeat the following mantra.

SAA: Infinity, cosmos, beginning

TAA: Life, existence

NAA: Death, change, transformation

MAA: Rebirth

Duration of the mantra should be around 3 to 4 seconds.

This cycle meaning Creation from the Infinite or higher forces comes life and existence.

After life comes death or Change/Transformation.

Back in to the rebirth of consciousness.

Positioned in Gyan Mudra and changing with each fingertip touches in turn with the thumb

while firmly pressing.

SAA, touch the first finger.

TAA, touch the second finger.

NAA, touch the third finger.

MAA, touch the fourth finger.

Your chant will be in three languages of consciousness.

1. Human Chanting in a normal or out loud voice. (The physical world)
2. Lovers Chanting with a strong whisper (The longing to belong)
3. Divine Chanting in the mind silent (Infinity)

Follow in sequence 1,2,3 Chanting 5 minutes on each mantra and repeat for as long as comfortable to do so try to push yourself further each time.

Can cause Headaches from an imbalance of energy build up. If you focus on the energy leaving from the third eye Centre of the brows on Each mudra.

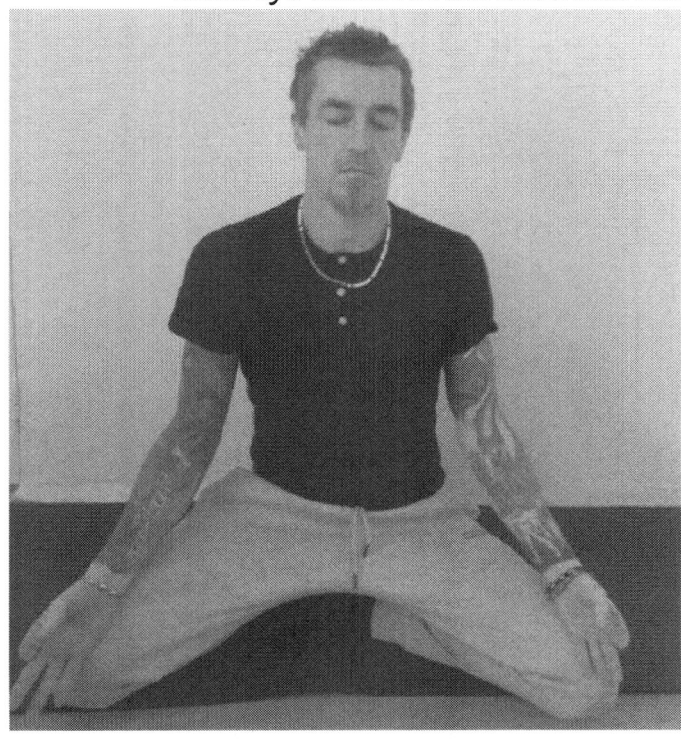

SAA (Knowledge)

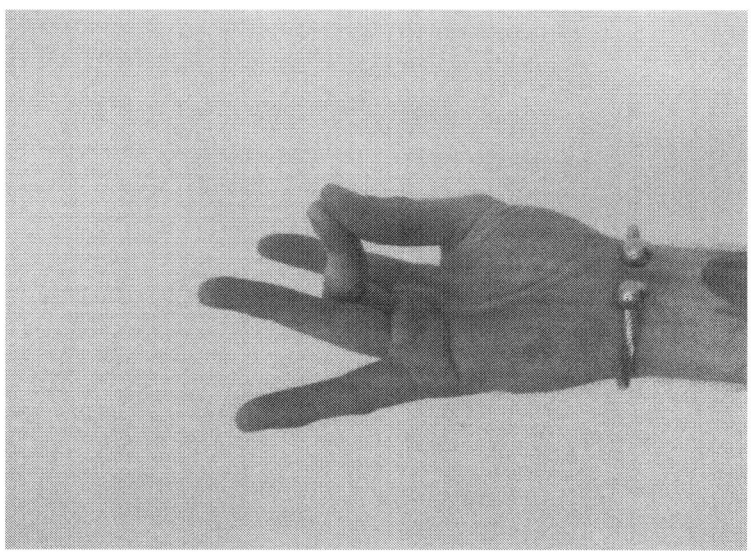

TAA (Wisdom, intelligence, patience)

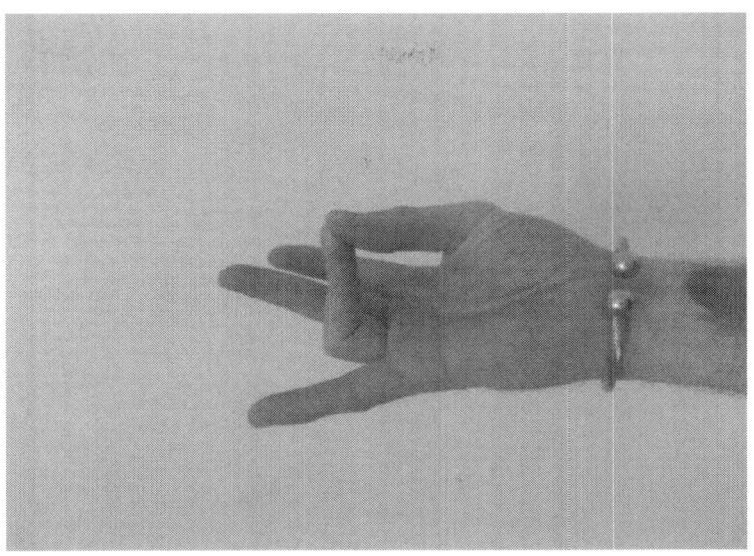

NAA (Vitality, energy of life)

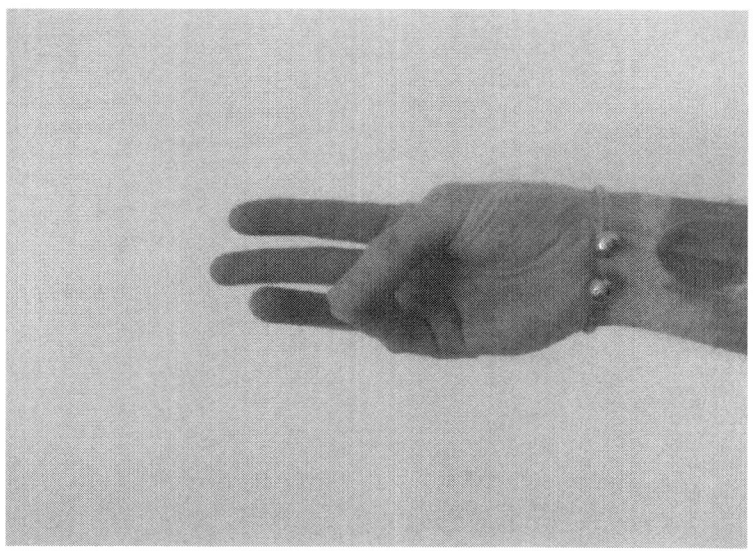

MAA (Ability to communicate)

CROSSING THE HOUR OF DEATH

Sit with the spine straight crossing over right and left hand at a 45% angle making an X.

Holding the hands around 6inches from the face. Start taking long deep breaths. Making them longer and deeper as you go on while Gazing at your hands and focusing on following the breath. Begin to turn your eyes up towards the centre of your brow while breathing from the bottom of the ribs.

5-½ Minutes.

This is called crossing the hour when the breath becomes hard. Known as the solid breath

were the lower side of the lungs become inflated.

Keep breathing hard through the mouth really pushing it. Close your eyes and visualise your

soul leaving the body through your crown.

Keep breathing up to 3-4 minutes Hard.

Then releasing the breath falling Down on to your back placing the hands on the heart

centre.

Now start sinking Deeper and Deeper releasing the body and your awareness.

Consciously passing out Sinking and dying as you keep going deeper and deeper.

Spending 30 minutes.

Play Sat Nam Wahe Guru While you let the body go deeper.

https://youtu.be/w0f5icFtXpk

When you die you have no choice of the ground you get.

This is knowing as dying in consciousness letting the body go from the mind.

Clearing any fears of Death or the unknown.

Separating the mind from the body letting the senses of the body die so you can travel on in

the mind leaving the body behind.

Feeling of the body being taken away swallowed up by the earth as the mind takes on its

own path not sensing the body.

Letting your thoughts go as the thoughts come from the earth with the body and now you release the body and the thoughts letting the body sink deeper and deeper down in to the earth.

The lower the body gets think of you just going in to light as the body sinks deeper and deeper the light becomes brighter and brighter.

You come to a place where all you can see is a dazzling bright clear light.

Now you have to sides or paths you can go one being warm and cosy were the other is cold

and icy.

Start heading down the dazzling icy path freezing with a reflection of glowing light and snowing with blinding light from it. Sensing none of it as you left your body and now all you see is the beauty and you keep moving on through the path.

Moving like you are a body like the body you left behind moving future down the icy path with glowing snow.

Now feel what it's like you have that body as you walk on through a valley of light without any senses a body would have you feel nothing just walking in a body with no senses.

Letting go of any senses a body would have.

Come to sit up the spine straight eyes still closed and playing Gong

10 minutes

Below is an example Any music you can relate to the exercise will work.

https://youtu.be/5L8hct4XFdE

Bring back your awareness of your senses resurrecting lifting up the physical body with the feeling of being here and now.

Listening to the sound feeling a wholeness with it and it as your power.

Finishing of with a deep inhale holding from 30-60 seconds and exhaling.

3 Times.

Then inhale deeply and hold for a 1 minute and exhale

And lastly inhale deeply hold for 30 seconds and exhale and relax.

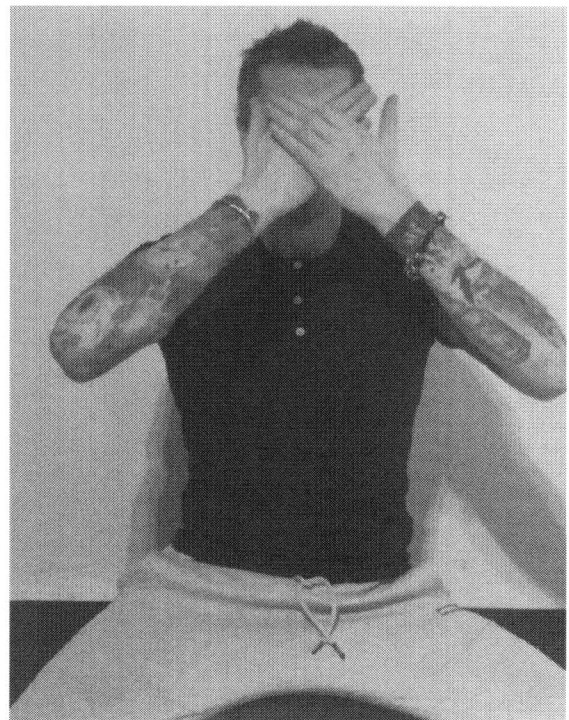

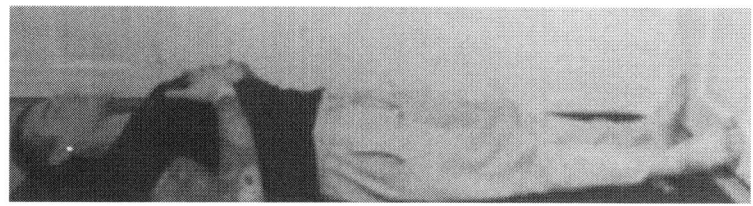

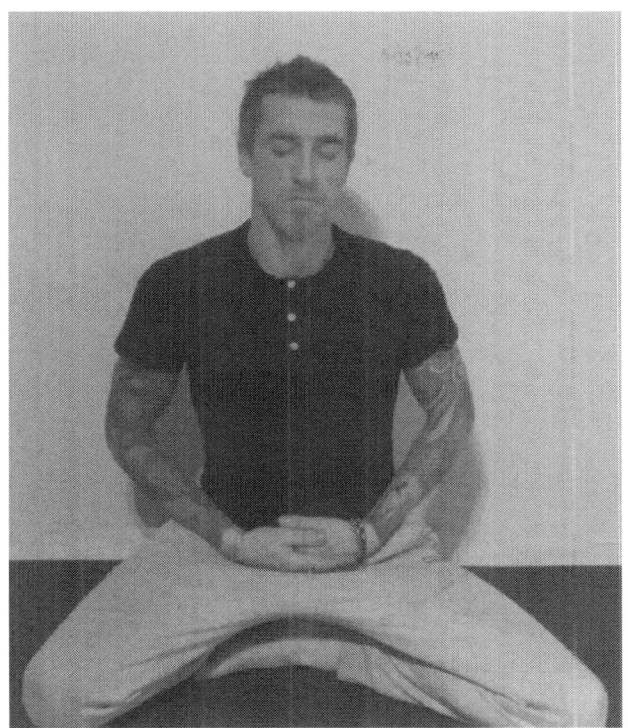

GRACE OF GOD MEDITATION

Lie down on your back with your eyes closed and relaxing the whole body.

For a woman She Should use the Mantra: I AM GRACE OF GOD.

For the man he should say: I AM IN THE GRACE OF GOD.

Inhaling deeply holding the breath and chanting Silently 10 times.

Also 10 times when exhaled the breath. Repeating this 5 times.

Come to sit up with the spine straight. Bringing the right hand in to Gyan Mudra (Index finger

pressing of the thumb).

Holding the left hand up by the Left shoulder with the palm facing forward.

The breath should be relaxed at a normal pace.

Going through the fingers on the left hand one at a time Starting with the little finger working the way to the thumb which will be last, tensing while the others stay relaxed but straight.

Meditating the governing energy for each finger and repeating the mantra 5 times.

Little Finger- WATER: Power to relate and
Communicate (with oneself)

Ring Finger- FIRE: physical health, Vitality, Grace and Beauty.

Middle Finger- AIR: Emotion to devotion and Patience.

Index Finger- ETHER: Wisdom and Expansion.

Thumb- EARTH: Positive ego.

Finish of by Meditating silently for a few minutes till your read to get up.

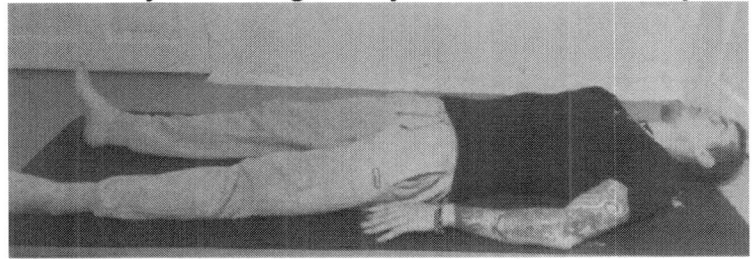

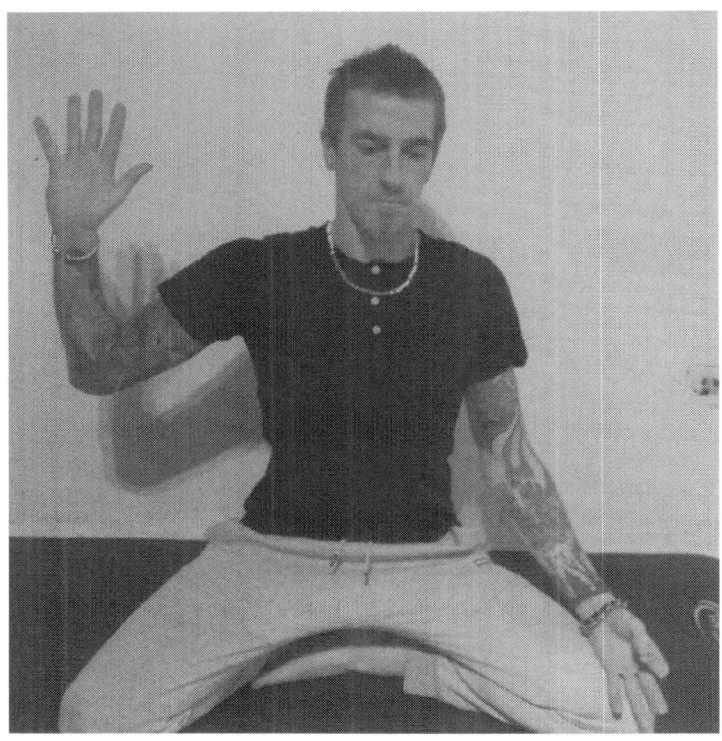

MEDITATION FOR
A CALM HEART

(Apply jalandhar bandh at the end of the book
(body locks))

Sit with the spine straight
and Eyes Closed.

Placing the left hand on the centre of the chest heart centre with
the fingers pointing to the

right and parallel to the ground.

The right hand should have thumb and index finger pressing on
each other held by your

shoulder with the palm facing forward.

Being conscious of the breath and guiding it inhaling
slow deep breaths through the nostrils.

Holding the breath in raising the chest and keeping
the breath held for as long as possible.

When ready exhaling slowly and smoothly making
sure you exhale every bit of the air out.

Then hold the breath locked out for as long as possible.

Build yourself up to 30-40 minutes

End the exercise with 3 Strong deep inhales
and exhales forcefully.

Now relax.

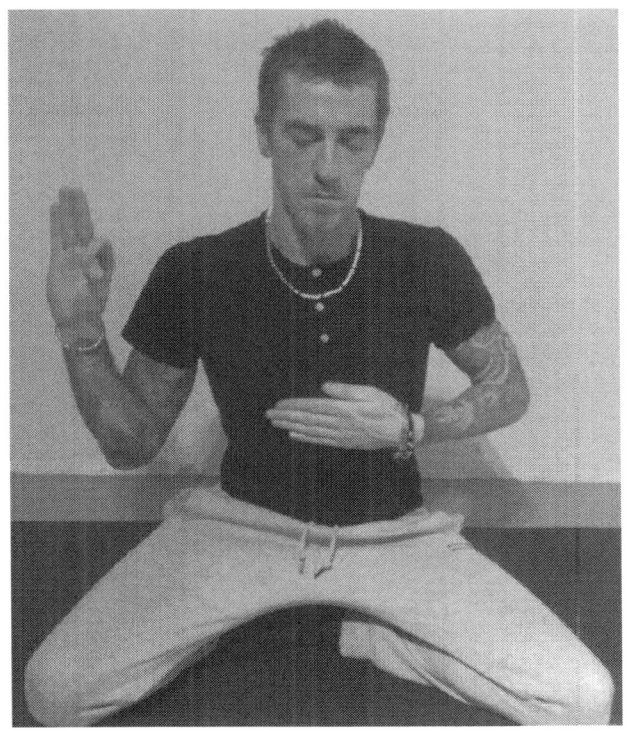

MEDITATION ON THE DIVINE MOTHER

Sit with Spine straight and eyes closed.

Thumbs and index fingers pressing on each other the Gyan Mudra.

Now Meditate visualising Infinity energy spiralling without the beginning or without end Extending out to infinity.

cupping the hands by the side of the face around the sides of the eyes.

Start to beaming a bright clear light out between your hands visualising with eyes closed.

Out into infinity. This is very mind curing and you will grow to love the experience you get from it making it a very enjoyable practice.

While focusing take long deep slow equal breaths. As you go deeper into the meditation begin to chant Saa, Taa, Naa, Maa

Guide your reason to go through the powerful circle you've created between the hands with that beam of light shining out from you like a head lamp.

While focusing on the beaming light your sending out Chant the Kundalini Mantra:

AADEE SHAKTEE, AADEE SHAKTEE, AADEE SHAKTEE, NAMO, NAMO,

SARAB SHAKTEE, SARAB SHAKTEE, SARAB SHAKTEE,

NAMO, NAMO,

PRITHUM BHAGVATEE, PRITHUM BHAGVATEE,
PRITHUM BHAGVATEE, NAMO, NAMO

KUNDALINI MAAT SHAKTEE, MAAT SHAKTEE, NAMO, NAMO

Can practice 10 minutes up to 1 hour depending
how you feel just know to push yourself.

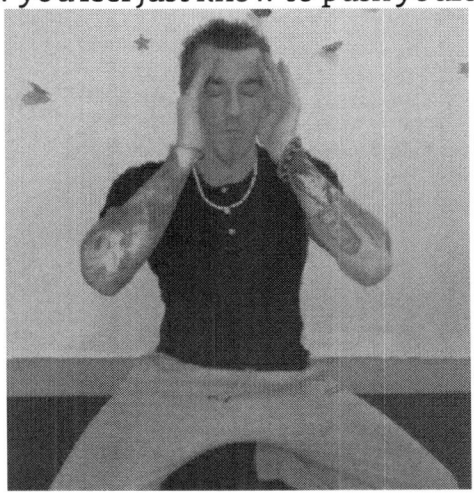

This Meditation Gives Concentration and mental beaming.
Tuning in to the frequency of the Devine mother.

The primal, protective, generating energy.
Taking away your fears and fulfilling your desires.

Removing any blockages of insecurity, you may have.

FOR HEALING
ADDICTIONS

(Apply jalandhar bandh at the end of the book (body locks))Sitting with the spine straight eyes closed focused of the centre of the eyebrows.

Now lock in your first 6 vertebrae by holding them out front tensing.

Clinching fists thumbs held up, now press the thumbs on your temples and the fists should sit nicely in to the head.

As you do this bring your teeth pressed together your molars in particular.

Mouth closed as you press on the molars release and press repeatedly while keeping the teeth touching at all the time.

You should feel the connection between the thumbs and the molars as you press on them.

Now vibrating the sound SAA, TAA, NAA, MAA focusing the sound at the brow point.

Practice from 5 minutes to 30 minutes.

Addictions are an imbalance just under the pineal gland that makes the addictions Seem unbreakable.

This stimulates this area directly underneath the stem of the pineal Gland.

Bringing balance to overcome the addiction.

BREATH AWARENESS

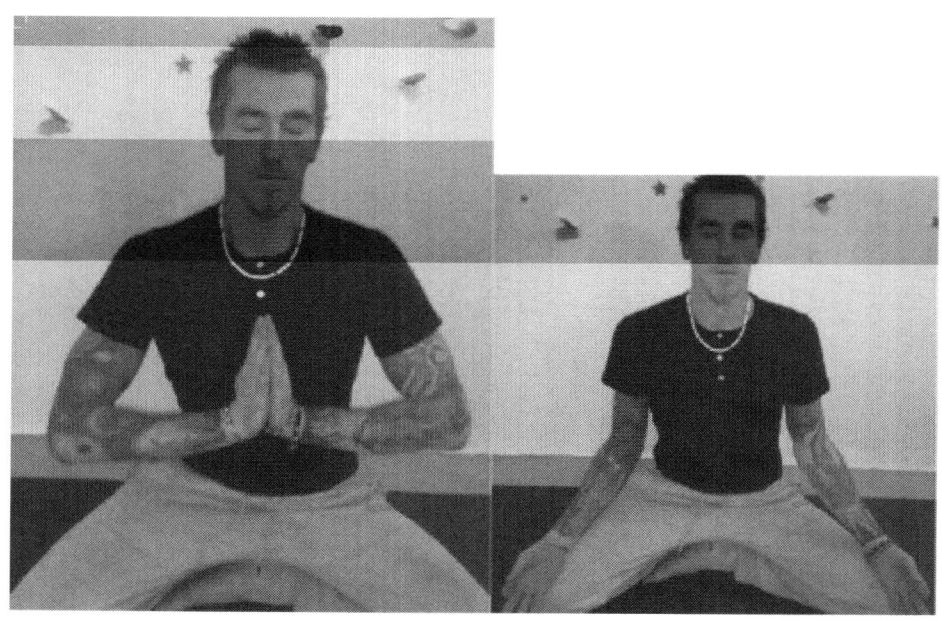

(Apply jalandhar bandh at the end of the book (body locks))
Sitting up straight in prayer pose or Gyan Mudra (optional).

Eyes closed focusing up in the centre of the eyebrows.

Feel your body balancing out as you breath.

Following the breath as it flows through the body sensing how the body changes as the breath hits in different areas of the body.

Keeping the breath at a steady pace naturally breathing.

Sense the breath filling you up with light as you and the breath become one pure clear light.

You begin to illuminate glowing brighter and brighter with a clear white light.

Connecting to the whole universe lighting up everywhere nothing but bright white light.

Becoming the universe letting it breath you feeling as one with everything a sensing wholeness.

The breath is part of a much greater force of energy which you are part of flowing through you.

Notice how the breath will change do not fight it or try to change let it take its path through you.

Appreciate it for the life it gives you with your awareness of its power and how it changes within you.

You should practice from 5 minutes to 1 hour long.

This brings about awareness of self and the force your connected to. Leaving you with an awareness to feel any changes in the body that may need attention where you can bring the breath to.

Avoiding illnesses and bad decisions.

It will also open up your awareness of others and your surroundings and how they influence you.

Think zero internally within as nothing but breath a flowing energy force running through you.

BEAMING AND CREATING THE FUTURE

Siting up with a straight spine and eyes closed while focusing on the centre of the eyebrow point.

Bringing the hands into Gyan Mudra resting on your knees.

Start of as if your drinking the breath and exhaling through the nostrils.

Carry this on from 7 - 15 minutes.

Then move in to inhaling the breath and holding it comfortably. While holding the breath thinking of Zero to any of your distractions from your senses. Zero to everything that takes your awareness away.

Exhaling when need to release the breath and repeating.

Carry this out for another 7 - 15 minutes.

Now think of the thought you desire most for your complete happiness.

Narrow it down to one word like Wealth, Health, Guidance, Knowledge, Relationship or Luck.

Then start beaming that word out from you as you focus at the centre of the eyebrow point seeing everything that comes with it and just follow the visualisations you beam it out from you.

Beaming your Desires.

This also should be done for a further 7 – 15 minutes

Listen to some frequency in the background will increase your vibration through sound 428Hz – 432Hz.

Relax now and lie down to take all in. You may get up when you feel good to.

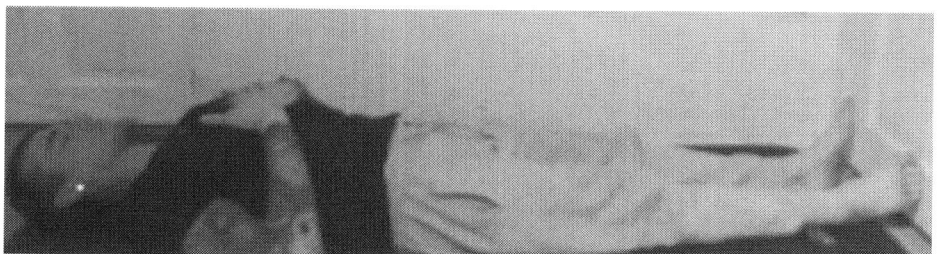

EMOTIONAL BALANCE MEDITATION

To prepare yourself you should drink a glass of water bringing around the awareness of the natural forces and water being the blood of the soul so to speak, with the majority of the body being water. What we have now in Science is shown how water carries messages, you should be able to picture how that relates to messages sent around the body with our senses.

Sitting with the spine straight and crossing over your arms in front of you.

Now turn your hands in under your arm pits hugging your chest thumbs held upwards.

Lifting your shoulders up towards the ears not forcing pulling your neck slightly back and dropping the Chin locking in the neck (Neck Lock).

Keeping the Eyes Closed while you meditate.

You can Practice this from 5 –15 minutes.

Just follow the awareness with the breath and in 2-3 minutes the feelings will begone from the thoughts the thoughts will still be there with no feeling to them.

Helping you in the future to any similar thoughts that come up and to be able to look at without catching on to a feeling towards them.

This Meditation is known as Sunia Antar.

It is said to be good for women but I would recommend to any-one with emotional attachments that does not serve you well.

Can be used in a moment when one feels like Screaming, Yelling and Misbehaving. For when you become out of focus with your emotions and let the ego take over.

As beings we are approximately 70% water and the relationship with water and earth in us earth Mater. There is an imbalance.

Normally we are rapid breathers with up to 15 breaths a minute that you most likely unaware of this mudra will slow the breath down a regulate the body balancing the breath with the body mater.

Try to bring the breathing down to four breaths taking long deep slow breaths. You will find just holding the mudra in position your breath will automatically slow down.

This takes away the obnoxious behaviour and calms the mind down.

No matter what the state of affairs is.

The kidneys become under pressure when there's a water imbalance in the body.

This can bring on a feeling of upset or worry within you.

By Drinking the water, you give the body what it needs to balance its self out and holding the mudra in place you cut of all connection to the brain. So, you will have the thoughts, but they will be separated from the feelings, until your body comes to a balance again with the help of the water and you continuing out the Kriya.

Very effective for the functioning of the brain.

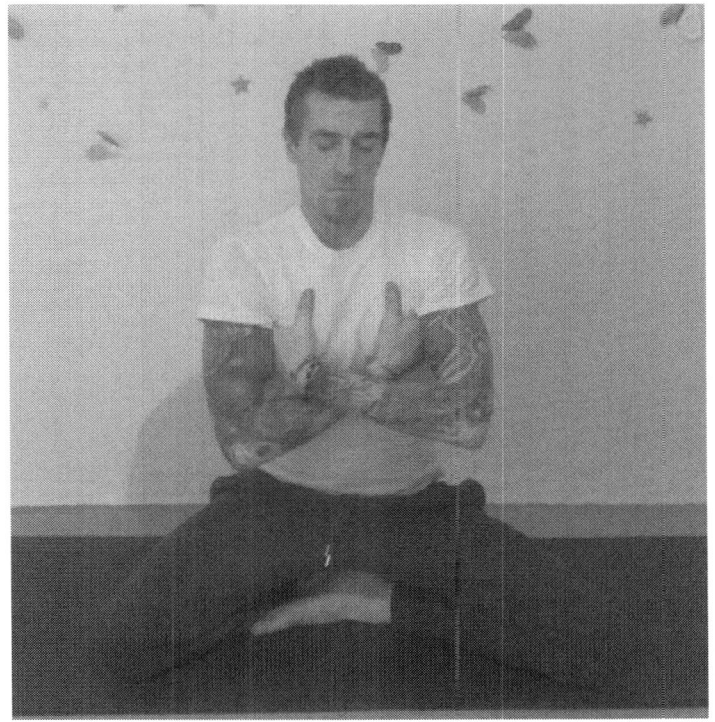

I AM HAPPY MEDITATION FOR CHILDREN

This is more for the kids over 6 years of age as any younger their attention span will most likely be shorter but for all ages and can be made fun were, they think there the adult with the practice. This is for when parents have arguments or when there's some disfunction going on in the home were the child can be affected.

This also can be done by anyone and can be fun to do.

Sitting up with the spine straight arms by your sides bringing the Hands up from the elbows and curling to fists with the index finger pointing.

Like when a parent would shake their finger to tell a child of.

Now you are the child would shake their fingers up and down like the parent giving out to the child.

Repeating I AM HAPPY, I AM GOOD,

I AM HAPPY, I AM GOOD,

SAT NAAM, SAT NAAM, SAT NAM, JEE

WHA-HAY GUROO, WHA HAY GUROO, WHA HAY GUROO JEE
This keeps the child stable from all going on around them so they don't be affected by the

surrounding forces.

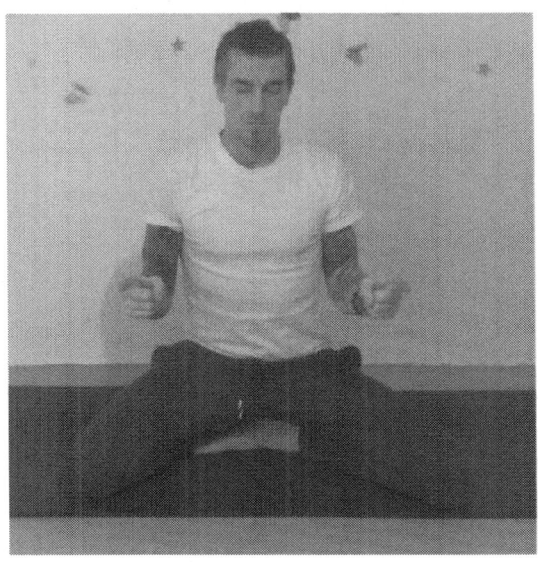

COMPASSION KRIYA

Sitting up with a straight spine, eyes closed and Crossing the middle fingers over the index fingers.

Singing along with Mantra

Rakhe Rakhanhar

https://youtu.be/EbgmgxGs2iQ

The first line of the Mantra: bring hands to the chest one hand over the other.

Keeping the hands middle finger over index and thumb placed at the base of baby finger as in the photo.

Second line: Lower arms resting the wrists on the knees.

Repeat as you go through the mantra arms coming to the chest on the last two lines of the mantra and as it starts again. Briefly lowering hands and back to the chest for first line again.

Carry out up to 31 minutes.

Compassion is the only beautiful thing which makes you human. When you take compassion from anything it becomes bitter.

It is a power of life it is truth giving you strength to go through suffering and yet feel no pain. You can find no grace without compassion.

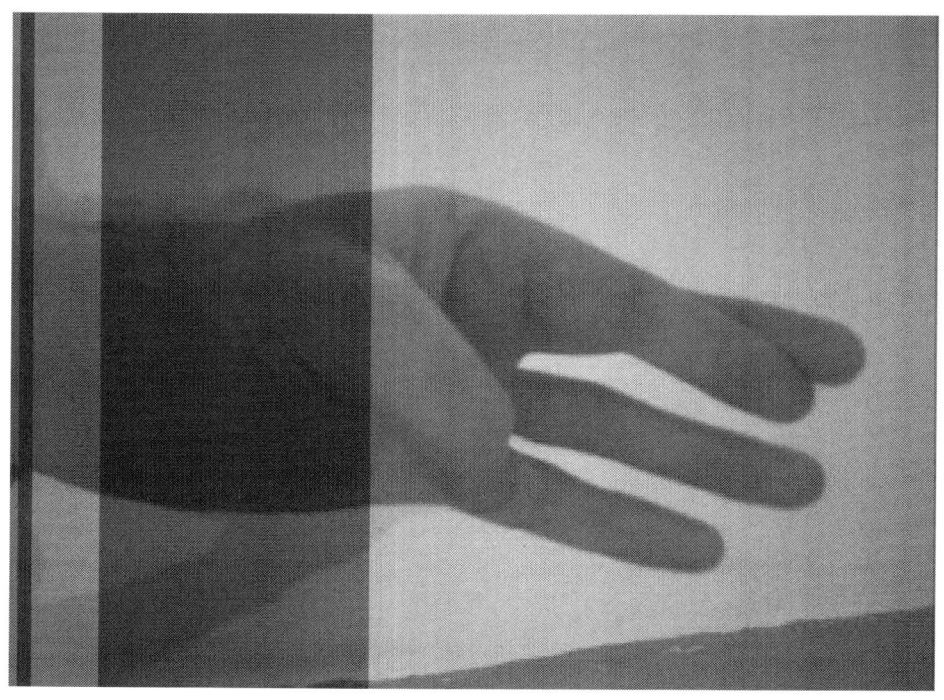

FIRING UP THE METABOLISM

Lying down on your back on something comfortable.
Bringing your legs up to point to the sky while reaching
up with your hands to grab hold of your toes.

How begin to open and close the legs and build up a rapid pace.

Do breathe a fire along with this getting in to a rhythm.

Carry on for 5 minutes.

Remaining in the same position now bringing
this to a rhythm with breath of fire also.

You want to Alternatively switch left and right feet
as you pull them towards you. Pulling on the left then
release and moving to the right and release.

Carry on for another 2 minutes.

Continue on for a further 12 minutes changing
the breath of fire to a chant Har.

So, when you move you chant Har.

Now combine the two movements.

Movement one opening and closing of legs and Movement two Alternatively pulling the left and right leg towards you.

Chanting har for when you pull the left leg to you and repeat har again when you pull the right leg in to you.

Then on the opening of the legs chant Mukanday Repeat this for 1-½ minutes.

Come to sit up and relax the body.

Now sit with spine straight arms by your sides bringing the hands up to the level of the shoulders.

Holding thumb and ring finger together with eyes closed and start chanting Har, Har Mukanday Carry on for 11 minutes.

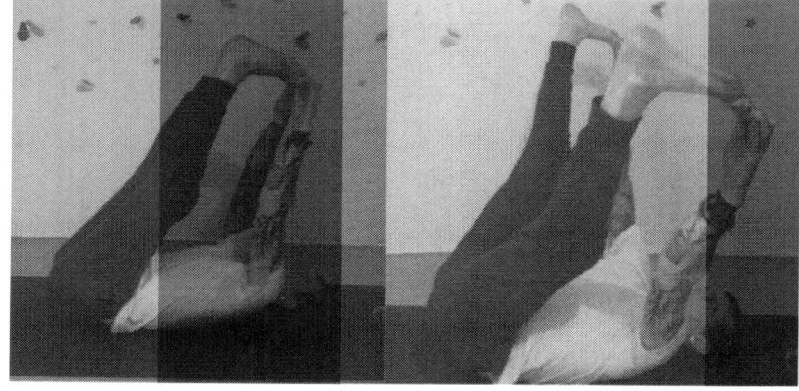

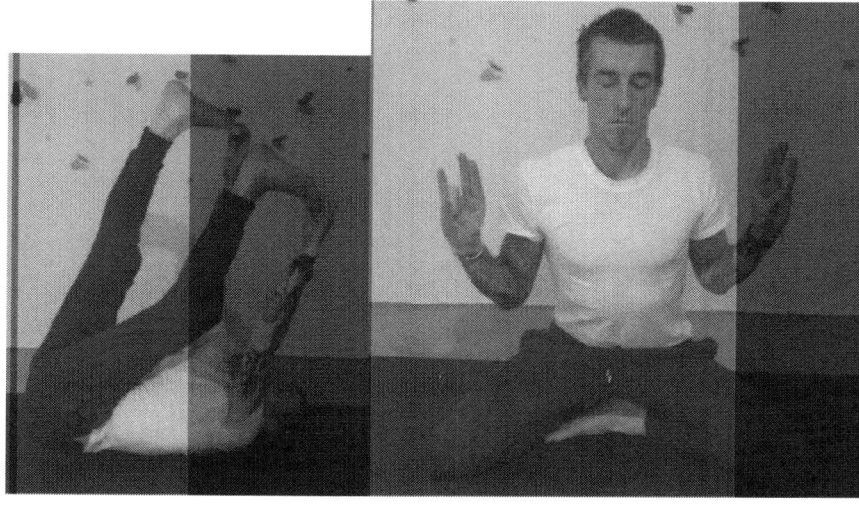

HEALING THE SELF

Sitting up with the spine kept straight crossing over your arms with the left arm crossing over the right placing your hands down on the opposite shoulder of each hand. The shoulders should hold the weight with the arms relaxed.

Keeping the eyes closed and focusing in the centre of the brows turning up and in.

Play: Ang Sang Wahe Guru.

Singing out from the tip of your tongue.

There are many versions of this song find one that is suitable to your liking.

Spend 30 minutes with this exercise.

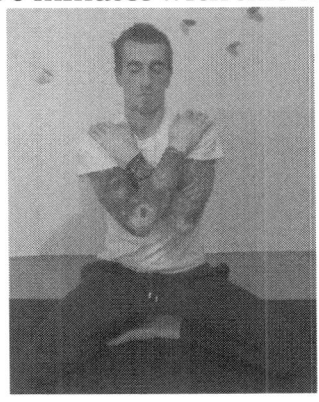

HOW MUCH YOU LOVE

A Male and Female Balance of Creativity Posture:

Holding left arm out 45% from the body bringing the hand up to shoulder level with the palm facing forward.

The right hand Should come straight out by your side parallel to the ground bending the elbow bringing the hand towards the side of the head the arm should now be in a 45% angle.

Now turning your palm out from the face sideways and the palm stays facing forward the bottom of your palm should be around eyebrow level.

Focus the eyes towards the tip of the nose and breath slowly while listening to Every Heartbeat.

There are many versions find one you enjoy.

Spend 15 minutes listening End with 3 minutes to go by stretch the arms straight up while you take a deep inhale holding the breath for 10 seconds.

Exhaling and relaxing for the following 3 minutes.

This exercise is for making you young the best gift you can give to the body.

Now keeping the spine straight with arms held out from the body in line of the shoulders.

Curling the forearms up so they are parallel to the ground and slightly wider than the upper arm.

Palms facing downwards with the fingers spread wide open stretching them out feeling the tension.

Begin to bounce the hands in a motion as if your bouncing a ball when left goes down right goes up and when right goes down the left comes up do this is fast motion.

The body will jerk.

Keeping the eyes closed looking up to the centre of the eyebrows

Carry this out for 8 minutes and keep the motion fast and powerful.

Finishing with a deep inhale tensing the whole body and releasing on an exhale then repeat 2 more times.

This exercise is for avoiding disease clearing the meridians.

Now bring yourself to baby pose with arms resting on the ground behind you with palms facing upwards.

Playing some soft music in the background.

Stay here for 4 minutes using the final minute to slowly come back up to your knees.

Final part

The Prayer

Sitting with a straight spine and arms held high at a 60% angle and slightly out in front of the body.

Palms are facing in at each other and the arms are stretched out locked straight feeling that tension as your reaching into the sky.

Now looking up towards the sky and close the eyes.

Spend 2 minutes here Trusting in your prayer.

Ask the Heavens and it shall be fulfilled.

Opening your heart with feeling and it will bring
all happiness and bliss you desire.

Love is your ultimate power being your
strength and not a weakness.

There's a lot of pain in love and that's life. But lovers do not feel it.

Life brings many pains but with god's love they give
strength to go on and smile laugh and enjoy.

AWAKENING THE INNER HEALER

Healing Sadhana to initiate the Healing Zone in you.

Healing energy is everywhere and within you when the Kundalini energy awakens it is called

Shabd Brahm –The Voice of God.

This is 10 Days to initiate your Flow of Healing.

Day 1 Do the Sushmuna Meditation
Day 2 Do Ida Meditation
Day 3 Do the Pingala Meditation

And the remaining 7 Days Chant for 1 and a ½ hours

SAA RAY GAA MAA PAA DAA NEE SAA TAA NAA
MAA RAA MAA DAA SAA SAA SAY SO HUNG

On the fourth Day start at 3am drinking nothing
but water or tea eating nothing for 20 hours, until
11 pm. then chant at 11pm to 12:30am.

From the 5th Day to the 10th Day Chant At any time of the day.

It would be good to always follow the next day where
you left of the day before 12:30-2am-3:30 and so on.

Day One:

sitting with the spine straight Chin tucked in
and chest held out. Spreading the mouth wide
with a smile showing the teeth with a slight
gap between upper and lower teeth.

Breathing rapidly in and out through the teeth.

Continue 5 to 11 minutes.

Opening the arms out at 60% palms facing upwards

Visualising a body of water wider then you can see.

Feel you are ready to jump in.

At this moment the power lies breathing slowly and
deeply 3 times.

This posture can transmute your sexual energy in to a
great purity.

Now Mentally leap into the water keeping your arms
up in the air.

You start going deeper and deeper till you hit the
bottom with tons of water over you.

Feel that water around you for 1 minute.

Inhale deeply and hold the breath relaxing the body
finding your body come floating to the top.

Letting it float on top of the water.

As the breath starts to shorten feel the lightness of it in you.

When you feel your crown begin to come out of the water
you will shoot up fast exhale and relax the body 1 minute.

Within 2 ½ hours after this you will experience the
effects of some special energy moving in the body.

Day Two:

Ida Meditation sitting with the spine straight and
left arm held out to the side at 45% angle.

Relaxing the hand so the fingers drop down.

Holding the right hand to the centre of the chest energy
centre keeping the arm parallel to the ground.

Holding the mouth in an o shape breathing
in and out rapidly through it.

Be forceful with the breath and continue 5 – 11 minutes.

Now bring your hands together at the Energy centre of the chest.

Hold them like a lotus.

Begin to meditate at the centre of the eyebrows
visualising the words HAR HAR WHA-HAY GUROO

Repeat them for 3 minutes.

Now focus on the lotus imagining a beautiful woman
covered with flowers and fine scents.

In the Ancient Tradition this was known to be Lakshmi
who was the goddess of wealth and prosperity, with
two white elephants placing garlands on her.

Feel filled with joy and spend 3 minutes combining both images.

Then come to meditate beaming pure clear light through the centre of the eyebrows projecting the light out.

Play the gong in the background and each time it struck visualise that pure light radiating out carry this on for 7 minutes.

Now repeat the starting exercise of day Two for 1-3 minutes.

Finishing with hands coming in to Prayer Mudra Placing and your heart energy centre.

Meditate focusing on your hands neutralizing your energy.

Listen to Naad.

The blessing by Sangeet Kaur.

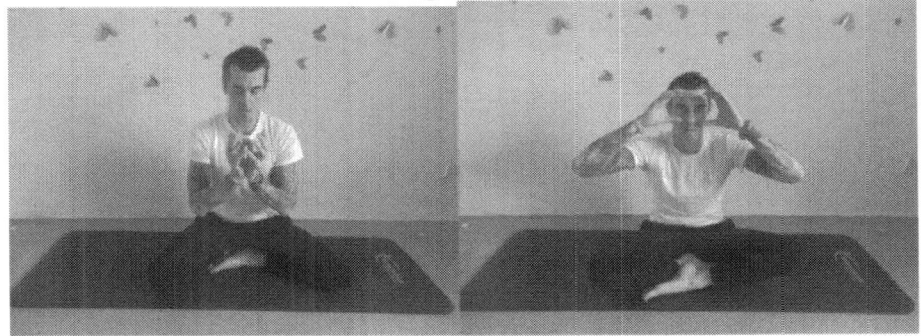

Day Three:

Pingala Meditation

Sitting with the spine straight holding your hands like you were holding a scope viewing from it.

Looking between the thumbs and the hands as you hold them out in front of the face.

Keeping the outside hand moving forward and back as if your extending the scope and bringing it back in.

While doing this you are doing breathe of fire.

Continue on for 7- 11 minutes

On the last 30 seconds close your eyes.

Inhale deeply extending the arms out making a 90% angle from one arm to the other.

Now see yourself as a great Eagle flying around enjoying the freedom breathing slowly and deeply.

Go way up in to the clouds.

Spend 7- 11 minutes flying around.

Inhale deeply with your wings spread out focus on the power at the tips of your fingers and begin flapping the arms up and down.

Do this in a fast motion as you inhale and exhale hissing your breath through the teeth.

Continue on for 2-3 minutes.

Inhale deeply and hold that breath till comfortable to release and exhale.

Repeat 2 more times.

Relax and open the eyes. Now put on some lively

music and sing along for around 5 minutes.

LONG CHANT

(Apply jalandhar bandh (At the end of the book body locks))

Sitting with the Spine kept straight

Hands in Gyan Mudra or you can rest them on your lap in each other.

There is only one creator of all creation and truth is the creators name.

Greater than any description with infinite Wisdom.

Inhale a deep breath pulling the Abdomen in tight to the spine.

EK ONG KAAR SAT NAAM SIREE WHA-HAY GUROO

Keep the same pitch and length of the words in the chant equal focus on the body as the abdomen goes in and out getting a rhythm to the chant with the body feel the chant flowing through you.

Duration 3 minutes to 2 ½ hours

Vibrate the Sound out your Nose so your vibrating the upper palate sending vibration as you chant to the head.

This chant is done in Aquarian Morning before the rising sun.

This is when the channels will be most clear.

You will be connected with a higher source.

You will be Liberated from the cycle of time and Karma.

You become one with the Divine.

This connects your soul and the universal soul as one clearing all energy points bringing a balance to the body.

SELFCARE BREATH KRIYA

Selfcare increases your energy and strength boosting the immune system and cleansing the body.

Sitting with the spine straight open the mouth holding it in a circle.

Placing hands over the heart centre right hand over the left which becomes closest to the heart.

Closing your eyes bringing your awareness to the body and were you place your hands.

Now for 5 minutes breathing like a canon

Canon breath forcing the breath out at a steady pace while focusing on the shape of the breath your sending out by the shape of your mouth.

Ending with a deep inhale and hold the breath relax the mouth and repeat in the mind

I am beautiful,

I am innocent,

I am innocent,

I am beautiful,

Exhale through the nose and repeat 4 more times then take time to relax.

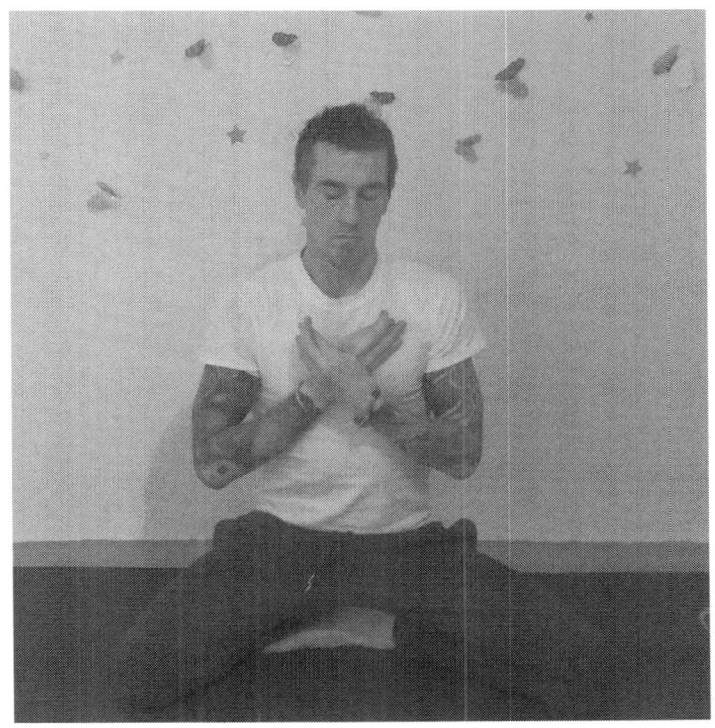

REACTING TO CHILDHOOD PATTERNS KRIYA

Sitting with the Spine straight.

Place your left hand at the chest level keeping the fingers straight with the palms facing right. Then with the right hand press the fingers into the base of the left hand's fingers.

The palms should be facing each other.

Thumbs resting along the side of other and the eyes kept shut.

Breath long deep breaths through the mouth breathing from the throat.

Continue on the breathing for 3-5 minutes.

Then take a deep breath at the end and hold it keeping the awareness of the body's energies moving hold for 1 minute.

Any thoughts or feelings you want to release gather them up and release them out the mouth like an explosive canon.

Settle the breath then repeat this process 4 times in total.

Kept satup with the spine keep straight bring the hands to the front of the shoulders with the palms of your hands facing out in front of you.

Left hand: Thumb and baby finger pressing at the tips on each other.

Right hand: Thumb and ring finger pressing
at the tips on each other.

Eyes Closed and begin breath of fire through the mouth.

Carry on up to 3 minutes at the end of the three minutes
take a deep inhale holding up to 30 seconds.

Focusing on the top on the head.

Do this 4 times in total.

Now Cross your hands on your heart energy
centre right hand on the left.

Bringing your eyes to focus on the tip of
the nose with the eyes closed.

Breathing to your natural rhythm of the breath.

Meditate feeling from the heart with a
sense of totality and vastness.

At peace with any thought or persons that come to your
mind bless them. Bless yourself and any thoughts.

Come to Gratitude bringing in the sense of light Scanning
your childhood ever year up to 11 years old bring in the
light with kindness and blessing to each memory.

Sense what happens as this time is cleared and released
with the force of the light.

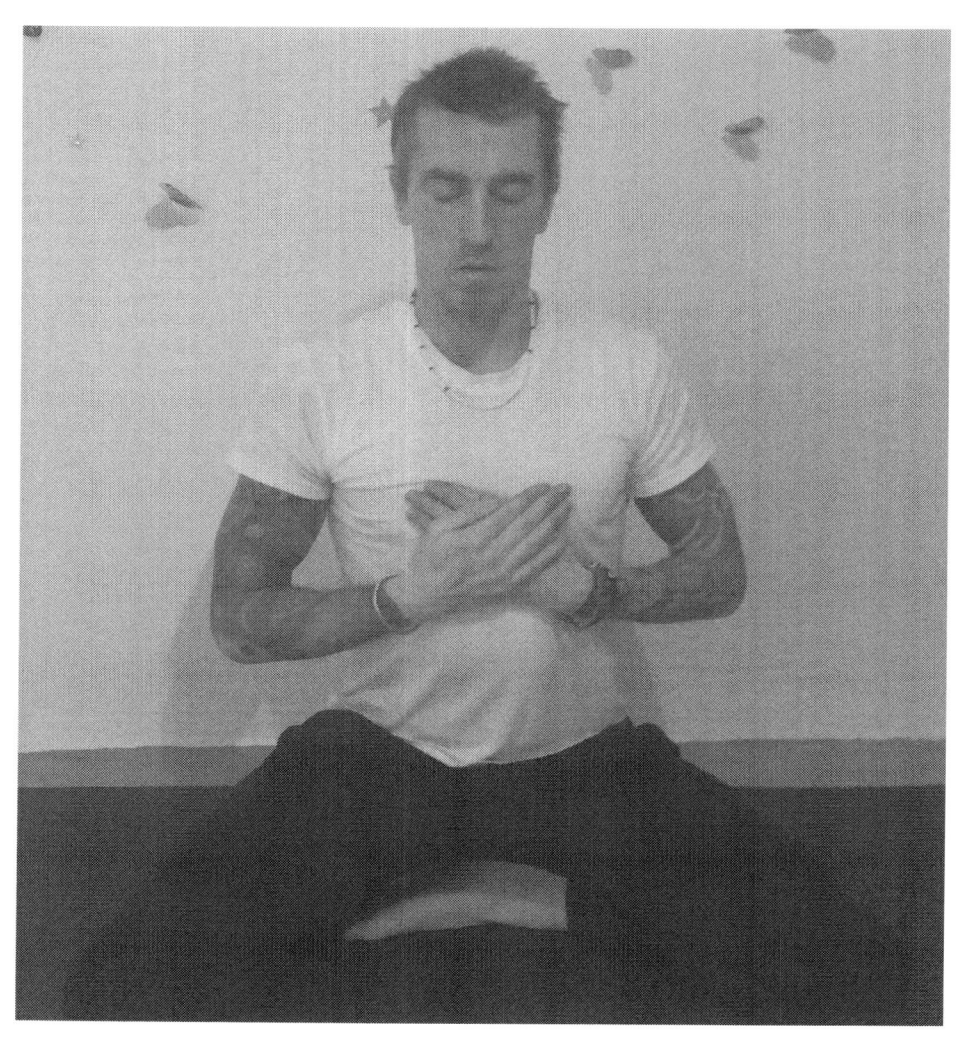

MEDITATION TO
CHANGE THE EGO

(Aplly Jalandhar bandh(at the end of the book (body locks))

Keeping the Spine straight and the chest slightly lifted up.

Arms by your sides bringing your hands up to
the chest curling up two loose fists.

Raising your thumbs to point upwards.

Bring together so the thumbs are pressing of each
other with the rest of the fists kept apart.

Keep your eyes focused on the knuckles of the
thumbs with the eye's half closed.

Now focus on the breath.

Bringing the breath to 4 equal parts with the

Inhale: 8 seconds

Hold: 8 Seconds

Exhale: 8 Seconds

Hold: 8 Seconds

The time can be increased but always keeping it Equal.

Do this practice from 3- 31 minutes

At the end inhaling deeply bring the hands over
the head opening and closing the fists several
times and relaxing down with the breath.

The practice identifies any attachments so you can
let go sending them out from you in to the universe.

You may hear sounds this can be pressure on the eardrums
adjusting in the skull.

This is bringing a normal adjustment in the
neurons in the cortex and will pass.

TEEN KRIYA – SANMUKH KRIYA

Sitting with the spine straight and eyes focused on the tip of the nose.

Bringing your hands up to shoulder height rolling in the ring finger to the base where it meets with the palm. Pressing down on it with the thumb.

Bring the Abdomen in tight to the spine and slightly tilt forward.

Holding this position meditate Silently
While you repeat the Mantra.

Mantra:

SAT SIREE,

SIREE AKAAL. SIREE AKAAL,

MAAHA AKAAL, MAAHA AKAAL,

SAT NAAM,

AKAAL MOORAT,

WAH-HAY GUROO

Continue for 11 minutes.

When perfecting this Kriya you and god will sit face to face.

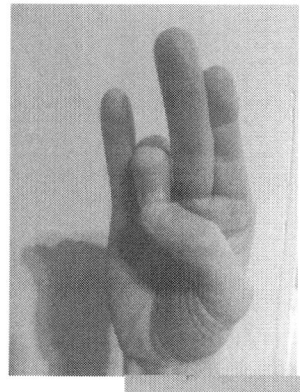

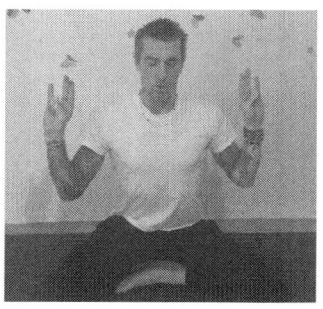

This will give you strength and take you away from weaknesses.

It will give you vitality. You may find you want to overdose on this meditation but do not go past 11 minutes the mind is more powerful for the body and it will need rest and may not be ready for the energy.

When you have this energy, you can move the whole world and you would not like to move yourself, you reach nonexistence and would ruin your life.

Second part:

Same posture as you began.

Begin to chant the mantra Wah-hay Guroo

Breaking it up in to two sections saying them separate.

WAH

(Together) HAY GUROO

Carry this out for 11 minutes.

When Chanting chant, it short and fast (WAH) pulling in sharply on the sexual organs (Root Lock) them.

On HAY you pull in more and up more locking in (Diaphragm Lock).

To remember HAY and GUROO are said in one flow.

On GUROO your applying in the (Neck lock).

Pulling slightly back the neck and dropping the chin slightly.

You keep going over this as you keep chanting.

Remember to release to start again.

This gives you a power to mover the universe.
When perfectly down and chanted perfectly you connect to the power of the third eye. You can guide

things to you with the power you create and fast.

Finish with the spine straight, eyes closed and Chin dropped.

Hold the chest out and interlock the fingers placing the hands behind the back of the head.

Don't drop the arms keeping them extended.

Chant:

SAT NAAM,

SAT NAAM,

SAT NAAM,

JI.

Carry on for 11 minutes and the relax.

KRIYA FOR GUIDANCE

Sitting with the spine straight and the eyes closed focus of the centre of the eye brows by turning the eyes in and up.

Playing Rakhay Rakhanahaar in the background.

Bringint the arms to cross over each other grabbing the forearms with the opposite hand.

Swinging the arms from side to side like rocking a baby moving slowly with the breath.

Taking 8 long inhales and exhales.

Then bring your hands into Gyan Mudra.

Now listen on up to 30 minutes, while slowly breathing to the music feeling the music within you.

Feeling a pulsating up your spine as you keep the navel tucked into the spine.

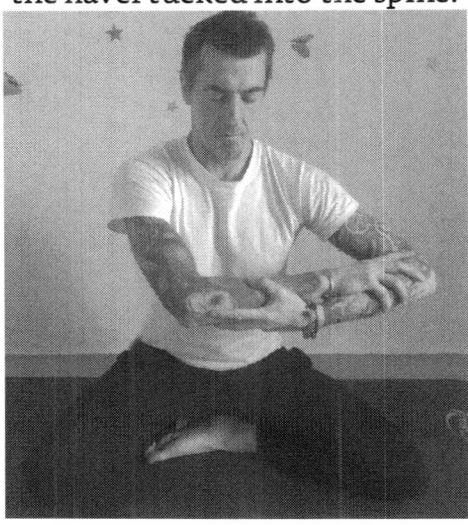

INNER CONFLICT RESOLVER REFLEX

Sitting with the spine straight Apply Jalandhar bandh (Find at the End of the Book (Body Locks)) and the 3 Body locks in place.

Closing the eyes focusing on centre of the eye brows or tip of the nose.

Placing your hands on your chest and placing your attention on the breath.

Each inhale and exhale should last for the count of 5 seconds.

On the exhale you should hold the breath out for 15 seconds suspending the chest as you pull in on the navel bringing closer to the spine.

Finish of with stretching the arms above the head and taking a deep breath o exhale shake the arms out and relax down.

Start with 11 minutes and work your way up to 60 minutes.

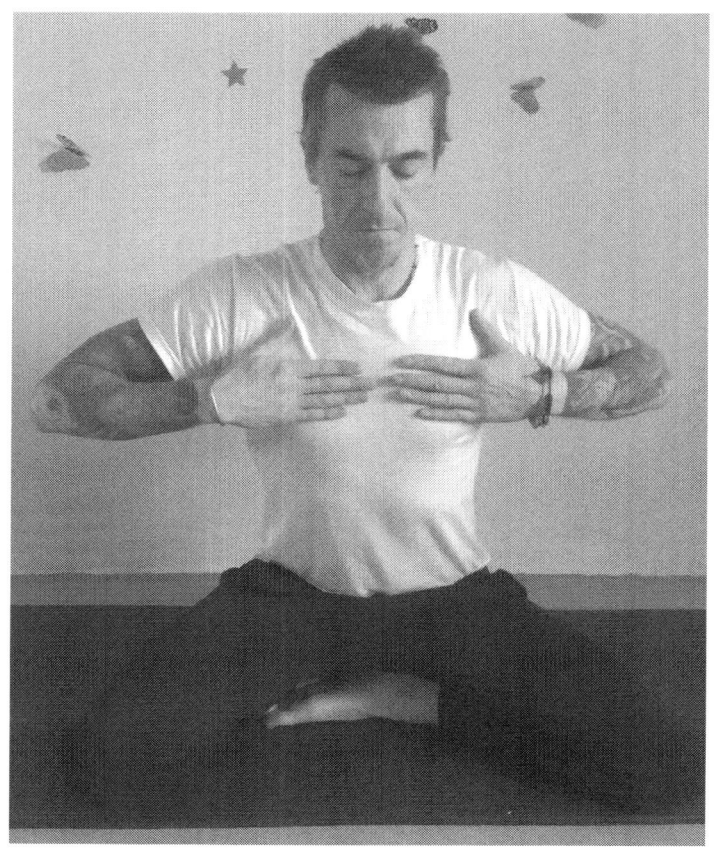

Any Kriya That has Jalandhar bandh.

This Means Body Locks.

This locks in the Energy in place as you build it up in your Kriya.

At the end of the Kriya you will release and all energy will shoot up the spine.

To Apply the locks.

Root Lock: You Suck up your sexual organs.

Diphram LockP: You pull the Navel in to the spine.

Neck Lock: You pull the head slightly back and drop

the chin the body should be locked now.

Youtube you can find helpful videos For Guidance

Mind Body Reprogramming

Innerheal

https://www.youtube.com/channel/
UCRqjJj5U9ZEDNxp2x6t76Dg

Or Add on Facebook

https://www.youtube.com/redirect?
event=channel_banner&q=https%3A%2F%2Fwww.face-
book.com%2FHooponoponoancientHawaiianhealing
%2F&redir_token=bv0uUyalsuTXGUVXxjmnnKRjB-
sJ8MTU4MDQxNjg4MkAxNTgwMzMwNDgy

Made in the USA
Columbia, SC
09 November 2020

24220542R00061